IT'S GAME TIME.

GAME PLAN

ACHIEVE YOUR GOALS IN LIFE, CAREER, AND BUSINESS

Ciara Pressler

All of these ideas have been expressed somewhere before. What's specific to this book is the unique culmination of my experience and my goal-setting approach. I created this book because I believe that the world's a better place when we're pursuing what we truly want and supporting each other along the way. So I encourage you to share it with your partner, family, friends, teammates, colleagues, club, elected officials, and anyone else who could use a swift kick in the strategy. However, if you want to use it as teaching material or in any way that is tied to profit, get approval first by emailing Ciara@CiaraPressler.com. Use your judgment, common sense, and integrity.

The material in this book is intended for educational purposes only. No expressed or implied guarantee as to the effects of the use of the recommendations can be given nor liability taken.

Published by Press LER New York City
First Printing, 2015
ISBN 978-0-9885135-2-5

Get more at CiaraPressler.com

DEDICATED TO YOUR FUTURE SELF.

CONTENTS

PREGAME

Several years ago, I invited a few friends out to brunch on New Year's Eve with a radical caveat: instead of the usual brunch agenda – divulge the latest gossip, vent about work, overanalyze our love lives, order one more round of cocktails – why not make it a productive encounter and attack those ever-dreaded New Year's resolutions? To sweeten the deal, I even offered to make a goal-setting worksheet.

To my surprise, people showed up. Eight of us dove enthusiastically into a different kind of resolution: not just thinking about what we wanted to accomplish in the upcoming year, but also celebrating the big and small things that had happened in the recent year while affirming each other's intentions for growth. A group of ambitious, in-demand, overscheduled New Yorkers took time to appreciate our own accomplishments, to consciously plan for what we wanted next, and to support each other.

While the supporting worksheets were made with a sense of humor, I knew the power that writing things down carried when it came to making a commitment. Not just throwing some goals on a sheet of paper, but strategizing an actual process to go from zero to complete.

In fact, I had created a career out of it, advising creators of businesses, creative projects, and even coaching services on how to transform their ideas into their reality.

That year, our New Year's resolutions went from nice intentions to actual accomplishments.

Thus, the New Year's Goal Brunch was born. Attendance doubled each year. I continued expanding the worksheets as new success principles became apparent, delivering a new edition at each event.

Realizing that these principles might work for more people, I published the worksheets on my website. It quickly became the most-visited page of my site, shared across social media and in person with friends, family, colleagues, clients, students, and anyone with an interest in finally going from thinking to *doing*.

It's proof of what we already instinctively know: there's something profoundly inspiring – and contagious – about locking in on your truest goals and making your own success happen.

We don't need new ideas. We need someone to sit alongside us and help us shape our ideas into a tangible goal and a corresponding action plan that is realistic, exciting, motivating, and perfectly tailored to who we are.

We need a Game Plan.

Let me rewind for a moment: I'm Ciara Pressler, and I work with idea people to create their strategic plans. They are entrepreneurs, corporate trainers, career coaches, film producers, fashion designers, music producers, authors, academics, real estate developers, tech innovators, fitness instructors, and lifestyle gurus. Since I've built a company dedicated to strategy, my commitment is to discover how success really happens – not just in theory, but in tangible reality.

Throughout my career, I've been fortunate to encounter an even wider range of very accomplished people: risk takers, business starters, award winners, record holders, ultra athletes, coaches, consultants, producers, creators. I pay close attention to their actions and how they approach their own goals so I can figure out what makes them successful. I devour every book, article, class, video, conversation, and resource I can find on how to do things better. I'm continually developing my goal-achieving process: identifying better ways to move forward and surrounding myself with equally motivated, curious, tireless doers. Discover, adopt, attempt, rework, improve, evolve.

Meanwhile, in my personal life, I take on projects: running nine marathons and over 100 races, producing events and fundraisers, writing books, traveling the world, and campaigning for World's Best Aunt, supported by personal development practices learned along the way. I'm hungry for new experiences and reaching my full potential.

In other words, I'm a bit of an overachiever and a big goal evangelist. Many years ago I realized that my life mission, the place where I feel most myself and in flow, is helping other people identify what they want to do and how to get on the path to making that desire a reality.

Strategy + Action: this means helping you discover your true goals *and* create a realistic system for success.

But this is not a standardized test. This is your older sister sitting you down after graduation to tell you everything she's learned thus far in an effort to make your life easier and more fulfilling, and to help you reach your dreams faster. Grab a beer and listen up.

This book is a combination of everything I've created, consulted, taught, learned, or otherwise absorbed to date. It combines all of my goal worksheets, as well as the best advice from my business and career articles, webseries, and book.

Let's get graduate-level on goal setting. Here is the process that has worked for me and for those I consider a success, both in work and in life. I'll keep revising it as I learn, try, succeed, fail, and get your feedback, because the best celebration of success is sharing it. Why hold onto something that can help someone else?

Full disclosure: I do not accomplish every goal I set. But I do make sure to learn just as much from my failures as I do from my successes. Instead of giving up or ignoring what's uncomfortable, I try to take note of what works, what doesn't, and why.

I've begun to notice that the foundation of goals that get accomplished, that are the most fun, and that are most central to making me who I am, have these three things in common:

1. Being honest about what I really want.
2. Being honest about where I get stuck.
3. Knowing myself well enough to use my strengths and plan around my weaknesses.

The common thread? Telling the truth about what I want and creating a realistic process to move forward. Honesty is the foundation.

The thing that makes my approach different is that I encourage acknowledgement of challenges, obstacles, and failures. This is where honesty gets difficult, but really earns its value.

It's natural to resist this. But ignoring the truth has a funny way of derailing your progress until you finally deal with it. So the logical, healthy thing to do is to deal with it now so you can discover what lies beyond.

Unlike most goal-oriented guides, this book doesn't stop at presenting best practices for goal setting. It also acknowledges that obstacles appear and encourages you to deal with them proactively, then develop a process that is tailored to your life, habits, relationships, strengths, weaknesses, and incentives. I do my best to keep it simple and straightforward, and to provide specific examples where it makes sense.

This is not "Dream it and do it!" I'm a skeptic. It's comforting to have a "ten steps to" doing/being/having whatever, but the only thing that matters is what works in reality. Second-guess trends. Keep what works and throw out the rest. This is the more difficult path, but it is the one that will actually move you forward.

Which means you might get uncomfortable. You might not like some of what I have to say. Pay attention to those moments: they can be opportunities to identify your blocks and expand your possibilities.

I invite you to dive into this guide, improved and expanded with new ways to set, analyze, adjust, and achieve your goals in work and in life.

Be honest. Be realistic. Be ambitious. Move forward.

Honor the opportunity you have to create your life by committing to your process and telling your fears that they're not invited to the party. You'll inspire others with your courage – and inspire yourself with the new things you learn and the experiences you create.

The point? We are more fully ourselves when we are in touch with what we really want and realizing our unique ambitions. We are kinder, more generous, inspired, and connected, both to ourselves and to others.

Strategy & Style,

Ciara

HOW TO USE THIS BOOK

This book is designed to be like Law & Order: SVU – self-contained episodes you can skip between and repeat, but that make even more sense (and are more fulfilling) when you consume the whole series in order. Also, a tough-love female detective is leading the discovery process, but you can't sleep through it if you expect to solve your mysteries.

The Strategy outlines 24 Goal Principles that will help frame all your endeavors. Because different areas may call for different approaches, there are separate sections for your **Personal, Career,** and **Project Goals.** That last category applies to you if you are a creator of any kind, whether you're working on a business, creative project, or event.

Below are suggestions for how to adapt this book to your style and schedule. You'll also need a pencil, highlighter, snacks, and a can-do attitude. The first three are sold separately.

WORKOUT
Interval Training
This book is ideal for quick reading and reference, from subway rides to delayed doctor's appointments. One-page chapters and separate goal sections mean you can formulate your Game Plan on your time.

GAME TIME
60 Minutes
Allow about an hour to work through each goal section.

CHAMPIONSHIP
2-3 Hours
Create a mini Goal Retreat: give yourself an uninterrupted stretch to complete your Personal and Career Goals. Be sure to find a space where you can escape distractions and get into your zone.

GOAL EVENT
3 Hours
Gather a group of friends or colleagues to formulate your Game Plan as a group. You can download a free DIY Goal Event packet at www.CiaraPressler.com.

TIME OUT
30 minutes
It's vital to check in with your goals regularly. Schedule a repeating 30-minute appointment on your calendar to give yourself time to refocus and realign.

HUDDLE
45 minutes
If you're working with a goal buddy or accountability partner, keep check-ins quick and efficient: take 20 minutes each for getting help with your goals, and five minutes for scheduling and next steps.

BE RELENTLESS. THE MORE SPECIFIC AND HONEST YOU ARE ABOUT YOUR GOALS, THE MORE LIKELY YOU ARE TO TAKE TANGIBLE STEPS TO ACCOMPLISH THEM.

STRATEGY

What does success mean to me?

→ Not what others would view as success
You can end up sabotaging yourself by trying for something you don't want.

RESOLUTION

HYPER-AMBITION AS ANNUAL TRADITION

Every year, trillions of people set New Year's resolutions and only about ten of those people accomplish them. *Literally.*

So it would seem that *setting* goals is pretty easy. Why is it that most goals we set never get *accomplished*?

In my experience, the first problem is the goal itself, which usually has one of these flaws:

- **The goal isn't specific.** When a goal is too general, you can't assess or adjust your progress.
- **The goal is too big.** It's not broken into digestible steps, causing you to get overwhelmed and give up.
- **The goal is too small.** It doesn't inspire or motivate you, so you ignore it in favor of other things that captivate your attention.
- **The goal's timing is off.** The goal isn't realistic for right now or is in conflict with another goal.
- **You have too many goals.** It's impossible to manage and act on everything.
- **The goal isn't something you want badly enough.** You're doing it because it's what other people are doing or what you "should" do, but it doesn't really resonate with what you truly want right now. Something else is more important to you in this moment.

When you start with the right goal, you stand a much better chance of accomplishing it. From there, planning, motivation, tracking, and accountability, along with a healthy amount of self-awareness, take you the rest of the way.

REALITY

CHECK YOURSELF BEFORE YOU WRECK YOURSELF

Spoiler alert: there is no formula for success.

I'm sorry to break the news. But we all keep buying into this idea that if we just take the right class, hire the right guru, or read the right book, we will be showered with fame and riches and respect.

I'm guilty too. I repeatedly get seduced by the latest theory, program, article, or method that promises elite results. But the only time these things actually contribute to my success is when I selectively apply some (not all) of the concepts to some (not all) of my projects. No single book or guru or TED talk has ever laid out an approach that I could follow to the exclusion of other information in order to reach my goals.

The absence of ten-step plans, detailed timelines, and specific roadmaps in this book may be frustrating, but a cookie-cutter guide that wants you to take the same approach as everyone else isn't going to serve you in the long run.

Instead, take responsibility for your own destiny and continue the development of your own unique approach to your life. It's more challenging terrain than simply following a map, but it will set you up for greater success and satisfaction.

Whether you are pursuing your goals alone or with outside support, it is up to you to think critically and make any process your own. Discover what works for you through trial and error. Throw out what doesn't work and keep what does. There is only one you, so there is only one unique path to your specific success.

Construct your personal success formula. Then continue adapting it as your goals require.

ENDURANCE

RUN YOUR RACE AT YOUR PACE

If you want to run a marathon, no trainer will tell you to get super-motivated and just leap out your door to run 26.2 miles all by yourself, and, if you can't do it, beat up on yourself and give up altogether.

Yet that's what so many of us do with our Big Goals: the long-term goals, the stuff that really matters. The finish line seems so far away that we freak ourselves out and stall at the starting line, self-sabotaging our way off track.

If you want to run a marathon, the best way to start is by getting up to a base of around 25 miles per week, or 5 miles x 5 days each week. That alone could take a year. Then you start inching up your long run -- 8 miles, 10 miles, 13.1 miles -- but with weeks where you pull back so you don't injure yourself by going too far or too fast too quickly.

You get the analogy. In order to accomplish a big goal, you have to divide it into smaller, more digestible steps. You need milestones in order to measure your progress, and, most importantly, so you don't get frustrated and quit because you're measuring yourself against a Future You that hasn't yet been earned.

I want you to be aware of your big goals, but take care to focus on each goal's respective milestones, which are often remarkable standalone goals. The trick is that you must choose goals that aren't just about the destination, but a process you'll enjoy.

If you hate running, do us all a favor and take a marathon off your bucket list. But, if you will treasure each mile and you're open to what you'll learn along the way, by all means, lace up and get focused on that first mile.

CLARITY

GET SPECIFIC FOR GOALS TERRIFIC

Lack of clarity is the enemy of goal greatness. Don't be vague about what you want. Strong goals are:

1. **Simple**. One sentence, simply stated, and don't smash other tangential goals in with it.
2. **Specific**. Get to the core of what you want and define it.
3. **Realistic**. This can happen within one year and is mostly within your control to execute.
4. **Measurable**. Make it trackable and give it a deadline so you can measure your progress.
5. **Honest**. Go for the exact thing you really want right now. Avoid "shoulds" and comparison.

My goals have a funny way of manifesting when I'm not specific enough about them. Either they won't work at all, or they'll happen like I stated them, but not always how I intended them. For example, one year I set a goal of saving $10,000. That amount did indeed get saved, but in my business account, not my personal one. Whoops, who cares, I had $10,000 more than I did that time last year. Fuzzy goals are rarely financially beneficial, so I need to keep a sense of humor about missing the mark. But when it really matters, what I really need to be is clearer.

Say you set a goal of saving money, but you are in grad school full-time and paying for it yourself. Plus, the interest on your debt would far outweigh the interest earned in your savings account. All things considered, is the savings goal realistic? Be honest about your priorities, as they are now, in your real world.

Original Goal:	*Save money.*
Potential Problems:	This isn't specific or measurable. How much money? One penny? One million? Do you want a raise? How much? What's your motivation? How will you do it?

Stronger Goal:	*I have paid off my credit cards by April 15 and I have $5,000 in my savings account by December 31 with a defined monthly savings plan in place for the New Year.*
Potential Obstacles:	Upcoming major purchases and expenses, bad spending habits, procrastination.
Action Steps:	Commit to saving a specific amount each week, set up a savings account, set up automatic transfers, use generic toothpaste, sell children to the highest bidder.

HONESTY

KNOW YOURSELF BEFORE YOU GROW YOURSELF

When I meet with a new client, *the goal they say they want* vs. *what they really want* are almost always two different things. Unfortunately, sometimes this doesn't become apparent until three months into the project, at which point the game changes when it might be too late. We've been moving forward fast in the wrong direction, so where we end up is much further from the real goal than if we'd been properly aligned at the outset.

How it went down before I created the Game Plan:

Client:	I want press on my business.
PresslerCo:	Great! We'll pitch your business story to media outlets.
	--three months pass--
PresslerCo:	Here is an article about your business in the newspaper.
Client:	Why aren't my sales up? I called you because my sales were down.
PresslerCo:	(*Slowly drops forehead to desk.*)

New and improved Game Plan approach:

Client:	I want press on my business.
PresslerCo:	What would you like your business to look like six months from now?
Client:	I would like my sales to be up.
PresslerCo:	Great! Let's create and execute a multi-faceted marketing strategy that builds your audience and empowers your sales.
	~fin~

Do you see how honesty about your real goals empowers efficient and effective action?

HAPPINESS

EMOTIONS WILL ROLL JUST STICK TO YOUR GOAL

There's something about the popular concept of happiness that's hollow, not to mention completely unrealistic as a permanent state. Life cannot always be a parade with rainbows and sparkles and that hyped-up cheerleader feeling, even if you get everything you want.

When setting goals, be careful to note where your reasoning is really "I'll be happy when…"

I'll be happy when I live near the beach.
I'll be happy when I get thin.
I'll be happy when I'm in charge.
I'll be happy when I have a child.
I'll be happy when I win an award.
I'll be happy when I retire.

When you chase happiness like an addict chases drugs, you end up being just as uncomfortable when the high is elusive.

Here are some emotions that are just as important as happiness if you want to be a complete and relatable human being:

- Curiosity
- Desire
- Sadness
- Anger
- Fear

All of these emotions have a function and they all pass eventually, so don't be too attached to their presence in order to do your work. Feelings aren't always facts. Don't abandon the plan just because you're not feeling excited about it on a given day.

Instead of happiness, pursue contentment. Inner peace. A spirit of service. The ability to withstand a storm without completely falling apart.

Set the bar at a realistic level so you can get down to the work of becoming the person you want to be.

CATEGORIES

NAIL YOUR TYPE TO DERAIL THE HYPE

Let's talk about HABITS vs. ACCOMPLISHMENTS. Most goals fall into one of these two categories, and you can set yourself up for success by acknowledging which category your goal needs to embody.

HABITS are things we want to make part of our routine: exercise, get to work early, floss.
ACCOMPLISHMENTS are events with a specific end point: take a trip, design an app, get a vasectomy.

(Why yes, grasshopper, some goals can be both!)

Let's look at that perennial fail, weight loss. One way of looking at the reason this goal almost always backfires is that people classify it under a completion (lose 10 pounds) instead of a habit (daily diet and exercise). This is where it helps to get honest about the real end-goal. If it's to eliminate your love handles before your beach vacation, fine, keep the completion approach. But if your real aspiration is to be fit, healthy, and energetic, craft a goal that outlines a lifestyle approach and creates ongoing habits.

With habits, let the practice be the accomplishment. Instead of giving up because you miss a week of hitting your habit goal, look at it as an opportunity to learn what sidelines you and what motivates you to get back in the game. Now the "failure" is reframed as a rest stop, not abandoning the journey altogether.

I recommend balancing your goal list with both types; you'll feel a sense of satisfaction from the completions, while becoming a better you by building the habits.

There's one more type of goal: **CHARACTERISTICS**. Similar to a habit, you may want to build qualities like compassion, honesty, or gratitude. But who you are is defined by what you do, so create a goal that puts your desired characteristic into action.

MEASUREABLE

IF YOU CAN'T TRACK IT YOU WON'T HACK IT

If your goal doesn't have time attached to it, you are sabotaging the whole process.

Goals are not just about WHAT; they are about WHEN. Your goals must include a deadline or some other marker of when you intend for them to become your reality.

Vague Goals That Will Probably Never Happen or At Least Drive You Crazy In the Process:

- *Get in shape.*
- *Get a boyfriend.*
- *Get out of debt.*
- *Go back to school.*
- *Start a business.*
- *Write a book.*

Why are these goals endangered species? Because you'll feel guilty from the start. You'll be telling yourself "Lose five pounds!" and your subconscious will be all stressed out because it hasn't happened yet.

On the flip side, you might also find yourself procrastinating on it without feeling guilty: why hit the gym in January when swim season isn't until June?

Measurable Goals That Have a Much Better Chance of Happening:

- *Lose five pounds by March 1.*
- *Eat five servings of fruits and vegetables every day.*
- *Exercise four times per week for at least 30 minutes per session.*
- *Go to the gym at 6:30am every weekday for the next month. I get two "free passes" to miss this appointment each month, no exceptions.*

Eliminate the possibility of failure and watch how much better you get at getting things done.

CONTROL

ACCEPTANCE IS KEY TO KEEP YOU FREE

This one goes out to all my control freaks, reading this from their perfectly-arranged desks, iPhones full of productivity apps, and highlighters poised above this page, ready for war.

It's seductive to believe that you can control the world around you. But sometimes there's a thin line between going after your dreams and manipulating your environment so that everything always goes your way. And the latter turns out to be a lonely way to live.

My goal-setting used to be about controlling life because I was afraid. I would deny what I really wanted because it made me too vulnerable or prone to disappointment. So I set goals that I knew I could accomplish, that felt safe. If I knew how things would turn out, nothing could hurt me.

The flip side of that coin is that a lot of my actions involved trying to control life, and by extension, the people around me. NO VARIABLES. Then Hurricane Sandy hit New York City. I couldn't control anything for a whole week and I lost my mind. That was the beginning of my realization that I had to change my relationship to the world, allowing for a little more flexibility to circumstances and a lot more compassion toward myself.

Your approach must allow for life's unexpected events. You might get laid off. You might get pregnant. You might meet the love of your life. You might break your toe during a dance party at Pam's house. There's no shame in retooling or postponing a goal when circumstances shift.

This is why I advocate setting goals that are just as much about the journey as the destination. Or as Mary Kay Ash would say, "If you shoot for the moon and fail, at least you'll land amongst the stars." I'll take it one step further and say: make sure the spaceship has good snacks, a great crew, and a kick-ass soundtrack.

While being adaptable seems contradictory to important goal principles like clarity and eliminating excuses, it is not. It's about accepting reality, being humble, and staying adaptable.

MANIFESTING

COUNT ON MAGIC IF YOU WANNA FEEL TRAGIC

Let's clear up the confusion that has been wrought by the concept of a "law" of attraction. Popular books like *The Secret* promote the simplistic notion that if you just focus hard enough you can attract whatever you want is a fantasy at best and dangerous at worst. Its popularity is making people miserable, except for its peddlers, who continue to capitalize on the easiest bet in success culture: our own laziness and need to feel superior to others.

The problem with "You manifest your life!" and taking a valuable principle like personal responsibility to an illogical end is that it's a creative, mean, and potentially dangerous form of blaming. Bad stuff happens. That is the way the world works. Adding a cement layer of shame when you get cancer or you get assaulted or your loved one dies is not going to help you deal with the situation in a healthy way.

The flip side is denial. If you're sick all the time but you also take poor care of yourself and have a bunch of unresolved psychological issues, it might not be just bad luck. So this, like all things, is a delicate balance requiring a ton of self-awareness.

I do believe that what you put out comes back to you – in the realm of how you treat people, not in the realm of praying to Santa Claus for a list of things you want. And if you wait around for a bunch of good stuff you think you deserve because *you just want it*, you'll only become resentful and bitter.

Karma is not a giant cosmic checking account. Doing something good doesn't mean a corresponding good thing will come back to you. When someone offends you, it doesn't mean they'll have their comeuppance.

Karma is this: the way you behave and your internal motives become the reality of who you are and the world you get to inhabit. So if you are a shady businessperson and avoid paying people who work for you, you'll become paranoid that everyone is trying to rip you off and live in a world of danger. If you give money to a beggar on the street, you will instantly feel wealthier and even start to notice more abundance everywhere.

Isn't that wonderful?

Here's my current view on forces unseen: you are graciously given talents and opportunities. It is up to you to maximize both.

It's that simple.

ACCOUNTABILITY

YOU CAN'T #YOLO IF YOU FLY SOLO

It is so easy to deceive yourself. This is why you need an outside person to call you on your bullshit.

Chances are, you already have some accountability: a partner, best friend, personal trainer, therapist, business consultant, or career coach. It always helps to have an outside person who shares in your responsibility and your motivation to become a better you.

A good accountability partner, aka Goal Buddy:

- **Strives for objectivity.** This is by far the most important.

- **Does not need something from you.** This person is not seeking your approval, so your Buddy is not afraid to point out where your goals are weak or how you aren't being true to your word.

- **Is reliable.** If your buddy flakes on more than one call or meeting, drop it like it's hot.

- **Doesn't gossip.** Goal buddies are a sacred bond. It takes incredible honesty not only to identify what you want, but especially to share it with someone else. Don't gossip about your buddy's goals or obstacles or new hairstyle.

Here's how we do it at our annual New Year's Goal Event:

1. **Everyone picks a partner they don't already know well.** This is important because it prevents going into old stories about why their excuses are good because their boss and their absent dad and blah blah blah. They're also more likely to be objective and respect your time. Of course, if your goal is shared with another person, like your business partner or spouse, you can be buddies too.

2. **The partners share their goals.** They also help each other if the goals are missing vital elements like a timeline or a realistic probability of happening within that time frame.

3. **The partners schedule a regular phone or in-person meeting.** They make a commitment to check in monthly or quarterly and put it on their calendars.

4. **The partners stick to their promise.** They don't schedule over that commitment or peace-out because of distractions. If it's not working, they both acknowledge it and amicably find a new arrangement.

KINDNESS

IF YOU CAN SPOT IT YOU'VE PROBABLY GOT IT

Once you're on track to your goals, it can get really easy (and fun!) to notice where other people aren't accomplishing anything.

You're volunteering once a month = Everyone else is lazy and selfish.
You're hosting a party = Everyone else is lazy, selfish, and cheap.
You're a parent = Everyone else is lazy, selfish, and needs to like your Facebook photos more often.

I do this with people's personal qualities: Ugh, he is so opinionated about his political views! Ew, she only talks about herself when we get together to catch up!

Then I heard this cold-water-in-the-face truth: If you can spot it, you've probably got it.

In other words, the stuff that bugs you most about other people is usually something that bothers you about yourself. It irritates you because it's provoking an awareness about your own weaknesses or limits.

The solution to being judgmental toward others is to be kinder to yourself. Your goals should never be about punishing yourself, and, if it feels like punishment, it probably is. Fortunately, it's simple (though not always easy) to solve. The solution is not to remove the punishing activity, but to change the activity that causes you to want to punish yourself.

An example: I used to get past my hangovers by running a few miles. Sweat it out AND get more fit in the process? How brilliant I was: I had solved hangovers! But those runs kind of sucked. They made me queasy and less attentive at intersections and I probably smelled like whiskey. In the end, it wasn't the runs that needed to change. What needed to change was my partying habits.

It's like my friend Keeley said after our last Goal Brunch: "I've been stressing about how to wake up earlier, then my Goal Buddy said the obvious thing I had missed: 'You can't wake up earlier unless you start going to bed early.'"

Attack the root cause, not the symptom.

VULNERABILITY

KEEP IT REAL AND FEEL THE FEELS

Brené Brown is a human connection researcher. The key finding that catapulted her to self-development fame was the discovery that vulnerability leads to fulfilling and authentic connections. I watched her TED Talk at least ten times and then read both of her books, but this still didn't click as anything other than a nice theory. Then the most wonderful thing happened.

I told a roomful of people who I desperately wanted to like me that I suck at something.

At last year's Goal Brunch, I told the story of my marathon training pattern: every spring I'd start working out a bit more, then wait until the last logical minute to start my official training, then do the bare minimum to get in shape to run 26.2 miles, then fall off my workouts the moment the marathon ended and continue through the holidays and pretty much stop working out in any significant way, losing all my race-ready fitness. This cycle more or less repeated for nine years!

Well, a few months later my friend Flora told me that it made a big difference to her own goal process to hear that I struggle with my fitness habits. To her, I was a marathon maniac and therefore not relatable to someone still discovering her own exercise routine. Knowing that I still have to deal with motivation both on a daily basis and in the big picture made her realize that maybe hesitation didn't have to mean opting out altogether.

That conversation with Flora marked the beginning of the most vulnerable year of my life thus far. I began to learn that there is great power in admitting and sharing my struggles. It connects me to others and = gives them opportunity to support me, whether through practical guidance or a good old pep talk.

A fairy tale ending is not always great inspiration. It creates a chasm because it doesn't tell the whole story. What's really inspirational is owning up to your shortcomings, facing your inner vampires, being honest about reality, and sharing your journey.

LOVE

GOALS ARE FUN WHEN YOU LOOK OUT FOR NUMBER ONE

For years I heard variations on that old maxim that you have to love yourself first, but I never really *heard* it, you know?

Some goals are really an effort to quench a deep feeling of unease with oneself, of being unlovable. It's tricky because a goal based in unworthiness can appear worthy to pursue. Example: it's wonderful to practice healthy food habits, but when you practice by depriving yourself of food enjoyment and doing juice cleanses to punish yourself for a party weekend and obsessing about your high school weight, it's borderline insanity.

It's a completely different experience to pursue a goal out of love and possibility for yourself. When you are acting out of fear, the pursuit of the goal is a punishment for not being *enough*: thin enough, man enough, talented enough, successful enough, young enough, tough enough, lovable enough.

Let's start with the opposite of love: fear. Love is expansive, expectant, open, grounded, brave, patient, compassionate; fear is anxious, controlling, closed, paranoid, defensive, judging, isolating, makes things more complicated than they need to be, and often in denial of reality. The inner voice of love sounds relaxed, wise, and keeps things simple. Love's voice sounds like The Oracle in *The Matrix*. The inner voice of fear sounds like an intense, dissatisfied, unpredictable stage mom.

When you are acting out of love, you are engaging possibility based on who you really are and how things really are at this moment. You exercise because you want to feel good. You choose a hobby based on what you really enjoy doing. You leave a relationship because it has run its course and being alone is just fine.

So how do you learn to love yourself? Same as anything else: practice.

Listen to how you're really feeling in the moment. Don't be afraid of it and don't judge yourself for it, just accept it and let it pass, because it will. Pursue things that make you smile. Learn to say no and set healthy boundaries. Do nice things for yourself. Think of a person you love unconditionally and do for yourself what you would do for that person.

Then you will be full enough and feel complete enough to truly be there for and connect with others. You will make a meaningful contribution to the world around you because you won't be acting out of needing things from people. You'll be overflowing with love and have extra to give away.

100%

HOW YOU SHOW UP IS HOW YOU GROW UP

One thing entirely in your control is how you show up.

Positive people are always talking about how 90% of life is your attitude and I'm like "Ugh, cliché," but it's true.

When you decide to perform at your personal Level 10, you often discover a higher level of performance than you even realized you had. 10 is Full Engagement. 10 is Focus. 10 is Passion. 10 is Excellence.

As Don Miguel Ruiz explains in his book *The Four Agreements*, you should always do your best. But your personal "best" changes from day to day. If you're sick, your best will not be at the same level as when you're healthy, and that's okay. The point is to have integrity around your effort.

Then there's the time part of showing up.

Here's a simple formula to find focused time to work on your goals: schedule one hour in your calendar each week at the same time and pledge to hold it as sacred as you would if you had an appointment with a valued mentor. Use this time to determine what needs to be done, develop your strategy, and schedule any actions you need to take in the upcoming week.

Then create a task list of things you can do in those slivers of time that are normally unproductive: during your commute, after lunch, while watching late-night TV. Turn those random 15-minute blocks into opportunities to get the busy work done.

If you have a hard time sticking to it, bring in an accountability partner, coach, or consultant to keep you honest. Isn't your productivity worth it?

COMMUNITY

FIND YOUR CREW TO DO THE DO

Once you begin to open your possibilities and expand your vision, you'll quickly have an epiphany: other people know how to do stuff better than you do!

When I finally started to understand the immense wisdom gained through open and honest experiences with a group of like-minded people, I started becoming the person I want to be a whole lot faster. Being around people who have similar values reinforces who you are.

If there's one area where goal gurus agree, it's that you have to watch your back in terms of who else has it. The people you surround yourself with have a ton of influence on you, whether you realize it or not. Is your environment supporting your goals or somehow undermining them?

Now, I'm not sure I agree with the maxim that "you are the average of the five people you hang out with most," much less disposing of friends who aren't the exact embodiment of the person you're trying to become. Different people bring different dimensions to your life, and it's incredibly rare that one friend or family member or colleague will be all things to you at all times. Plus, everyone goes through a rough patch or even an annoying phase. So while it's important to opt out of genuinely toxic relationships, let's always give each other the space to be human and evolving.

Here are some questions I ask myself about the people I allow into my life:

- Does this person love me whether I'm successful or just average?
- Does this person show up when I need them?
- Do I trust this person?
- Is this person happy and healthy?
- Do I have to play a certain role to be around this person?

Studies show that the happiest people are those in a dynamic community. So make sure your goals incorporate other people and that your success doesn't happen in a vacuum. It's better to do a little less with more love than to do more all by yourself.

JEALOUSY

OBJECTS IN MIRROR ARE CLOSER THAN THEY APPEAR

You don't have to be a hip hop fan to know one immovable law: haters gonna hate.

Like countless rappers before us, we too are going to encounter haters. Why do haters hate? Ah, the age-old question. Here's my take:

- **They're jealous.** They want what you have and it's easier to insult your courage than to construct a plan of action for themselves.

- **They're stuck.** Uh oh! Someone else is moving forward while they sit around complaining and blaming everyone else!

- **They're insecure.** You know that "friend" who always needs to feel superior? Topping your story, ignoring your contributions, turning compliments into insults. This is junior-high level hating.

- **They're lazy.** The need to feel comfortable all the time can be a dangerous goal-blocker.

Shake it off. When someone throws you shade, don't throw it back. Let it drop to the ground and walk away.

Hold on – what if you're not the player, *but the hater?* Let that sink in for a minute.

If you find yourself experiencing jealousy, be grateful. Jealousy is an excellent arrow straight toward what you want for yourself.

Here is the thing everyone I'm jealous of has in common: they are taking action on a goal I want for myself that I'm not pursuing with my best effort. Life, love, money, travel, work, writing, fitness, aunthood; no matter the area, I've learned to pay attention to my jealous emotions because they're clues to areas where my goals or actions are falling short of what I truly want.

ADVISORY

KEEP YOUR GOALS AWAY FROM THE TROLLS

Did you know you have an Advisory Board? Everyone does.

Your Advisory Board can be conscious – your business mentors, networking group, or even a formal organizational board. But your Board isn't limited to the people you actively ask for advice. It is anyone you allow through your mental filter and thus allow to influence your actions, beliefs, and perspectives.

For each goal or area of life, determine your Advisory Board: who has the insight, experience, outlook, and results you want? Befriend them, observe them, and consult them when you hit a plateau.

Be picky about your Board of Advisors. Get clear on which people you ask for which advice. In addition, be proactive about filtering out information that's not actually going to serve your goals.

Make sure the person who's weighing in actually has good and accurate information on the topic. If your friend has been in the same midlevel job for 10 years, she's probably not the person to ask about entrepreneurship. Your financially illiterate cousin is not the person to consult on Traditional vs. Roth IRAs. See where I'm going with this?

Here are three simple questions I ask before I embrace someone else's point of view:

1. **Does this person have the results I want in this area?** Don't ask your every-day-is-casual-Friday friend what to wear to a black-tie affair.

2. **Has this person actually gone through it or been part of a similar process?** Don't ask a serial employee how to start your side business.

3. **Is this person happy and healthy?** Don't ask a miserable person how to have a fulfilling experience. Also, life is too short to deal with miserable people.

That last one is key, because your goal is just the destination. Since the path toward your goal is where you'll spend the bulk of your time and energy, it should be full of people who make the journey easier, better, and more inspired.

EXCUSES

CASTING BLAME MAKES YOU LAME

When you're stuck, it's too easy to blame a perceived lack of resources. There's not enough time, money, or help to get ahead, right?

Right?

Let's use time as an example. "Busy" is the most popular excuse for getting out of responsibility, but it's also one of the most dishonest. Are you actually too busy or are you mismanaging your time?

"I'm *sooo* busy!" is a humblebrag. It isn't typically said to apologize or own up to mistakes; it's said to garner sympathy or opt out of a result. When a business contact tells me s/he's *sooo* busy, what's really going on is usually one of these four things:

1. **You're saying you're busy to sound important.** That's old-school bragging. New school is having a balanced and interesting life.

2. **You're not managing your time well.** Stop checking email every six seconds and log off of your social media accounts. Schedule fewer meetings. Force breaks so you have no choice but to finish tasks in between.

3. **You're not delegating.** Hire capable people and stop micromanaging. Make them responsible for succinct reporting and effective outcomes.

4. **You're not outsourcing.** If it takes you a whole day to update your finances, get a bookkeeper. If it takes you overnight to write a press release, call me. Understand which things are important for you to execute vs. oversee.

We make time for the things that are most important to us. So have integrity and own up to whether you're really busy or just avoiding doing the right things with your valuable time and energy.

Can you see how this might roll out to other areas? If you tell people (or worse, yourself) that you don't have enough money or the right partner, does it become the perfect excuse to get out of accomplishing goals?

What could happen if you removed your excuses? What could you achieve if you took complete responsibility for your success?

DISCIPLINE

START DOING AND STOP POO-POOING

A writer I know posted on her blog to complain about other writers who were getting published, even though – *gasp!* – they were worse writers than she. I didn't buy it. Art is not a merit contest; few things are. It's about hustle.

How did I finish my first play? Having the discipline to write down all my ideas and get into production.

How did I finish my first book? Writing every single day until I finished an entire chapter, even if it sucked.

How did I finish my first marathon? Putting one foot in front of the other, even if I was tired, unmotivated, or my training partner had other plans.

Of course you should strive for excellence. But excellence doesn't live in a vacuum – your editor or coach or teacher needs someplace to start in order to give you constructive feedback. You can absolutely maintain creative integrity and still start producing.

Perfection is the enemy of the complete. Doing always trumps thinking, and it certainly trumps complaining.

When I was writing my first book, I started a daily blog just to get in the habit of hitting the publish button. I needed a tool to break my habit of overthinking and procrastinating in order to get to that first draft. It not only worked, it affected all my work.

Identify your priorities and stick to your plan. Yes, of course, Life Happens. But you know what happens more often? Excuses. Kick your own ass into gear and have integrity with your process; only then will results start to appear.

OBSTACLES

BE INVENTIVE INSTEAD OF PREVENTIVE

Daymond John, founder of FUBU and investor on ABC's startup investment competition show *Shark Tank*, tells the story of his early days growing the clothing brand. There was very little money for production, let alone marketing, so they had no choice but to get creative. That innovation-under-fire led to guerilla initiatives that established FUBU, growing it not just into a multimillion-dollar empire but an iconic brand.

Ironically, more than one entrepreneur has said to me, "If I can just get this idea in front of [Daymond John or Other *Shark Tank* Investor], I'll be set!" I can guarantee you that this is not true if it's only an idea. Daymond and every other wise investor are looking for proof: is your idea so good that it can get momentum on its own? Are you the kind of founder who turns obstacles into opportunities?

One of the most pervasive problems that arrest a project's progress is burnout. We expect to get successful faster than is realistic and as a result, don't plan well enough for what it will take to build success over time. It's not just money. It's allotting enough time, energy, teamwork, and other important resources.

What is your idea worth, and are you giving it the support and resources it deserves? Creators routinely make choices that aren't optimal when focusing on cost instead of value. Crowdfunding a month's expenses or cutting corners by getting a friend to make your website for free won't generate reliable results, and you'll just end up starting over sooner than you'd expect.

If you want others to value your work, shouldn't you do it first?

When we don't start with a strong and realistic strategy, playing defense results in too many questionable decisions made in moments of desperation. Instead, the best moves eschew emotion and rely on wisdom gained from experience, market conditions, expert guidance, and common sense.

Like any healthy portfolio, your investment in your goals must carry a diversity of resources, people, growth strategies, and revenue sources. If you can handle enormous risk, fine, bet the farm on a single opportunity. But, if you're like most of us and want the maximum probability of a reliable return, balance it all with a multifaceted approach.

At some point, you'll indeed need help. Find it at the right time with the right people who will support your vision with the resources it truly needs to grow.

ACTION

AVOID PARALYSIS FROM OVER-ANALYSIS

Is there anything worse than wasting time trying to make a decision, only to realize you would have been better off just getting started sooner and figuring out the rest as you go?

Barry Schwartz's book *The Paradox of Choice* explains this truth: options bring freedom only to a point, and after that, they cause stress... or worse. We approach life as either Maximizers (I must have the best!) or Satisficers (I'm good!), and suffer or prosper accordingly.

It's easy to imagine how maximizing could wreak havoc on your personal life, constantly comparison-shopping your decisions about things of little consequence. Schwartz's advice is to take decision stress out of the little things (breakfast, workouts) to free up space for the things that matter (careers, partners).

Too much choice can lead to analysis paralysis, lack of decisiveness, and second-guessing one's (often accurate) first instinct. Taking action can be the best way to see if the road will be a freeway or a dead end. And then, once a decision is made, see it through – give it the resources, effort, and attention it deserves. Movement breeds momentum breeds results.

In most cases, action trumps analysis. Here is what I mean:

> Analysis: Spending 30 minutes browsing restaurants figuring out where to eat.
> Action: Going to the first place that will work for your needs.
>
> Analysis: Making a list of everything you want in a mate.
> Action: Going on dates.
>
> Analysis: Reading lots of books and articles about building your career.
> Action: Networking, networking, networking.

Over-planning can be a waste your time, energy, mindspace, and motivation, or even lead you to a choice that's way off-base. You'll create much better odds for your success if you get out there and actually try things vs. thinking too much about what you're going to try. Sometimes you can't figure out how to win until you're in the game.

PERFECTION

STRIVE TO PROGRESS NOT OBSESS

Perfectionism is tricky because it works. Until it doesn't.

When you're young, doing something perfectly is handsomely rewarded. If you get a perfect score on your test, then you can ace the class and be valedictorian and get into the top school and make lots of money and marry a trophy spouse and drive a luxury car and be your town's Richard Branson. Nothing can go wrong because you are the best and everyone wants to be you!

But perfectionism is alienating; it separates you from other people. When you can't accept your flaws or mediocre outcomes or just-okay days or come to terms with your basic humanity, it's really hard for people to identify with you. Relationships become a competition of sorting out who's best at what, or a hierarchy to reinforce your superiority, or an us-against-them team of perfection without deep connection. It really is lonely at the top.

Perfection is different from doing your best or showing up at your personal Level 10. Perfection is outside yourself, it is a construct of your culture. Being your best comes from within and only you can define it.

Perfection can keep you stuck. When you set out to do something perfectly, you don't allow room for mistakes, so you stand at the starting line planning planning planning, and the over-analysis leads to paralysis. You never start because you don't know exactly how everything will turn out. The worst thing you can do with your goals is spend too much time planning them and not enough time acting on them. You'll be mad at yourself for not unlocking the right formula and frustrated by your inactivity. It's even worse than not having any goals at all. (At least if you have zero goals you can chill out at the beach with zero guilt.)

Some days, I have to consciously tell myself: Go for a 9. When I'm aiming for 10, nothing can ever be complete because perfection is impossible. When I go for a 9, I create something excellent but I let myself off the hook of unrealistic expectations.

Aim for progress, not perfection. What's the next best step? Keep your eye on the prize, but realize there's no reward for standing in place.

SERVICE

SHARE YOUR WEALTH TO STAY IN HEALTH

If you're reading this guide, chances are you're fortunate to be blessed with the time and energy to contemplate your goals, plus the resources and capacity to move toward them.

We know we're luckier than many people, we say it all the time, but we rarely acknowledge this in practice. I challenge all of us to do at least one tangible act of generosity each quarter as an action of gratitude for our own opportunities, talents, and potential.

Below are some ideas; add your own and use the chart to commemorate your contributions.

- Sign up with a volunteering clearinghouse like New York Cares or HandsOn Portland to get access to thousands of volunteer opportunities
- Donate your gently-used stuff to a local charity or family in need
- Donate money to a nonprofit that does work you believe in – check CharityNavigator.org to find responsible organizations with good track records
- Buy coffee or food for someone on the street
- Mentor someone who is starting out on your career track
- Spend time with someone who's going through a rough patch
- Get creative – there are hundreds of things you can do to support others

WINTER	
SPRING	
SUMMER	
FALL	

PERSONAL
GOALS

★

Personal goals are where true success begins. Your priorities and values power your entire life: relationships, career, health, experiences, accomplishments, and even the unexpected occurrences for which you don't plan.

Your personal goals must come before career and business. Do not live to work; work to live. A few of us are fortunate enough to have careers that align perfectly with our personal passions, but that is not a requirement for contentment or joy.

There are a whole lot of people out there (and talk shows and magazines and, yes, self-development books) telling you to *Do! What! You're! Passionate! About!* – and that's lovely, inspiring even. But the follow-your-passion proverb can create an enormous amount of pressure. If your passion fades, a lack-of-passion attack is only going to block you from discovering what's next.

Here's the thing: passion changes. What we loved to do when we were younger may have served us then, but a dynamic life involves growth and evolution. Does a wonderful, even life-defining early experience necessarily have to dictate your entire life?

Some passions simply don't translate to careers. Many people are passionate about being parents, but that certainly doesn't mean they must become professional nannies. What it may mean, however, is that their ideal job allows them to spend meaningful time with their kids, to make the money that will allow that time to be minimally stressful, and to be able to leave work at work so they can be fully present as parents.

You don't necessarily have to do what you love *professionally*. Your foremost passion does not have to be your entire career or how you spend every day. I know this goes against everything everyone has been telling you, especially if you're American, were born within ten years of the eighties, or have ever opened a lifestyle magazine. If you love your children, does that mean you should be a stay-at-home dad? If you're crazy about tennis, will you be on the court at Wimbledon next year? Will I live in a Mexican villa with the cast of *Magic Mike* and a designer wardrobe and unlimited chocolate chip cookies and my own karaoke stage? (Please?) We have to dig deeper than the things that infatuate in order to discover the things that can give you a life you love.

The Game Plan is your opportunity to discover what matters to you at this point in your life. What are you passionate about today? Who do you want in your life? What do you want to explore, discover, or develop?

Set clear personal goals, standards, and boundaries. This will empower your professional life because you'll be a complete person, and thus better-equipped to take on any endeavor.

WHY IS A GAME PLAN APPROACH HELPFUL FOR SETTING PERSONAL GOALS?

In the Game Plan approach, we go big and then focus in on the immediate. You must give yourself time, and more importantly, *permission* to explore everything you want in order to determine the next best goal to get you there.

To make this process easier, we approach your personal life by category:

- **Self.** Who do you want to become? What traits or characteristics do you want to build? How do you want to develop spiritually? How do you want to relate to others?

- **Family.** How do you want to improve or develop your family relationships? How do you want your family to function and feel?

- **Relationships.** How do you want to improve your friendships? What do you want your love life to look like? What kind of partnership or marriage do you want to create?

- **Home.** Do you want to purchase a home, change your living situation, or improve the environment where you live?

- **Money.** How can you create current and future stability for yourself and those you support?

- **Experiences.** What do you want to do in your spare time? Where do you want to travel? What do you want to learn? What lights you up and puts you in a state of flow?

- **Wellness.** How can you best take care of your physical, mental, and emotional health? What is your personal health ideal?

- **Also...** What else? How can you live your own best life?

WHAT ARE COMMON OBSTACLES IN SETTING PERSONAL GOALS?

Take special care to avoid goals grounded in shoulds. Shoulds are anything that you feel you have to do based on your environment or culture, not what you actually want or need.

Shoulds can manifest in goals like:

- Going to business school because your dad wants you to.
- Getting a designer handbag instead of paying off your debt.
- Buying a house when it's really in your best interest to rent.
- Going to the gym ten times a week instead of moderating your sugar intake.
- Retiring early instead of finding work that contributes to your quality of life.
- Throwing the wedding of the century when a more intimate event would better suit you.
- Planning for a second child when you're really happy with just one.

WHAT ARE THE MOST IMPORTANT THINGS TO REMEMBER WHEN SETTING PERSONAL GOALS?

The point is to identify what you need in your life in order to be a healthy, happy, well-functioning human being. And to reiterate a vital point, the common thread between happy people from all walks of life isn't how much they accomplish or amass; it's the strength of their relationships. Create a life that allows you the capacity to build meaningful relationships and connect with your community.

Happiness is also a choice. Take pleasure in the little things and the unexpected moments, not just the standing ovations. Focus on the amazing experiences that happen every day and be grateful for what you already have.

It really is true that your attitude is what determines your experience. You can choose to drop the story of being stuck and, instead, regard yourself as powerful and full of potential.

IF YOU ONLY HAVE A FEW MINUTES

What GOALS do you really want to achieve more than anything else this year?

What specific **ACTIONS** will you take to get there, and when?

What **RESOURCES** do you need - things, people, time, etc?

What **OBSTACLES** are in your way, and how will you deal with them?

How will you know when you've reached your goal, and how will you **CELEBRATE** your accomplishment?

HELL YEAH

Write down everything that you accomplished in the past year. What were the top highlights? What are you most proud of? Pay attention to those that spark an emotional reaction. What makes your heart swell, your eyes light up, your face smirk in satisfaction? Nothing is too big, too small, or too weird. Go!

NOT RIGHT

What haven't you done that you really want to do? Where have you felt out of sync? What goals have you not accomplished and why? Why didn't you go for them? Were they too big for one year? Did you just not want them anymore? Did other goals or circumstances interrupt their progress? Were your blocks internal or external?

DON'T SKIP THIS. Finding the "why" behind the "didn't" will lead you to your solution, or at least a new next step.

VISION: LIFESTYLE

Brainstorm everything you want in your life, both short- and long-term, including accomplishments, habits, character traits, and experiences. Don't evaluate yet, just write down everything that comes to mind in each category, big or small. Have fun, no judgments!

SELF

FAMILY

RELATIONSHIPS

HOME

VISION: LIFESTYLE - CONT'D

MONEY

EXPERIENCES

WELLNESS

ALSO

PLAY

Go back to your brainstorm pages and pick your top priorities to attack or explore in the next year. You can choose one from each category, or just the top few that really capture your attention. It's too overwhelming to tackle 10 big goals at once, so be wise about only choosing what's important now, and then balance challenging with easy, big with not-too-crazy, "not sure" with "no problem."

Then use this page to mess around with the best wording for your selected goals - after all, you're going to be focusing on these a lot. The final version should be as simple and clear as possible, and, above all, be inspiring to **you**.

Write the final version of your goals on the fresh Personal Goals page, and then use the pages that follow to create your initial Game Plan for each one.

GOAL BREAKDOWN

On the following pages, list each goal and get specific about what it will take for you to accomplish it.

GOAL
What specific, trackable, exciting thing will you work toward and accomplish within the next year?

Pay off debt and save $5,000 by December 31.

MOTIVATION
Why this important to you now?

I've been meaning to save money for years and never do it, which makes me feel immature; I want to feel like an independent and responsible person; I want to buy a condo within three years.

ADVISORY
Who are the top people who can contribute solid advice and practical support?

Avery – bought condo last year and knows great mortgage broker
Ben – can help me rebalance my investment portfolio

OBSTACLES
What might stand in your way and how will you deal with it proactively? Having a strategy in place now will help you get back on track faster if life throws you a curve ball.

Invited to five weddings next year – write out expenses for each one and figure out if I can manage to attend all of them

ACTIONS + TIMING
How can you break each goal down into specific actions? Then – and this is vital –schedule specific times when you will put 100% of your focus on accomplishing these tasks.

Find out all my account balances and credit score – by January 15
Track my spending each week – Mondays 9-9:15pm (add to calendar)

CELEBRATE
How will you commemorate your accomplishment?

Spend a Sunday touring houses in my favorite neighborhood

★ PERSONAL GOALS

GOAL GAME PLAN

GOAL

MOTIVATION

ADVISORY

OBSTACLES

ACTIONS + TIMING

- [ ]
- [ ]
- [ ]
- [ ]
- [ ]
- [ ]
- [ ]
- [ ]
- [ ]
- [ ]

CELEBRATE

GOAL GAME PLAN

GOAL

MOTIVATION

ADVISORY

OBSTACLES

ACTIONS + TIMING

- ☐
- ☐
- ☐
- ☐
- ☐
- ☐
- ☐
- ☐
- ☐
- ☐

CELEBRATE

GOAL GAME PLAN

GOAL

MOTIVATION

ADVISORY

OBSTACLES

ACTIONS + TIMING

☐

☐

☐

☐

☐

☐

☐

☐

☐

☐

CELEBRATE

GOAL GAME PLAN

GOAL

MOTIVATION

ADVISORY

OBSTACLES

ACTIONS + TIMING

- ☐
- ☐
- ☐
- ☐
- ☐
- ☐
- ☐
- ☐
- ☐
- ☐

CELEBRATE

GOAL GAME PLAN

GOAL

MOTIVATION

ADVISORY

OBSTACLES

ACTIONS + TIMING

☐

☐

☐

☐

☐

☐

☐

☐

☐

☐

CELEBRATE

GOAL GAME PLAN

GOAL

MOTIVATION

ADVISORY

OBSTACLES

ACTIONS + TIMING

- ☐
- ☐
- ☐
- ☐
- ☐
- ☐
- ☐
- ☐
- ☐
- ☐

CELEBRATE

PERSONAL MANTRA

It's easy to get off track. A great way to bring your attention back to center is to have a saying that's inspiring, focusing, and true to you.

Use this page to create a mantra for yourself – what is your personal theme, slogan, tagline? Memorize it or put it somewhere you'll revisit it often: put it on your wall, make it your desktop screensaver, or perhaps create a needlepoint pillow of it.

CAREER GOALS

★

Now it's time to architect the next phase of your professional life. Rather than waiting for someone to hand you the career you want, you're about to empower yourself with a plan to create it.

HOW ARE CAREER GOALS DIFFERENT THAN PERSONAL GOALS?

Career goals can be particularly challenging because everything feels out of your control. After all, you don't decide who gets the promotion, whether you get a raise, if your company's stock price goes up, or if the customer buys your product. Or do you?

How would your job transform if you assumed responsibility for outcomes? Looking for solutions instead of dwelling on problems is the way to make progress.

WHY IS IT IMPORTANT TO SET CAREER GOALS?

If you have a college degree, you've spent around two decades and many thousands of dollars on your professional development. How's that for a hefty investment? And yet, when you enter the professional world, there's no master plan. Unlike the comfort of school with its built-in timelines and people whose entire job is to nurture your growth and success, you're now responsible for all of it.

A career Game Plan is your opportunity to write your own syllabus for the next quarter or year. What do you want to accomplish? How does it play into the big picture? Who will support your growth? Which actions must you take to get and keep momentum while balancing immediate demands?

Your Game Plan is insurance to protect the investment you have made in your career. Amazing careers don't just happen; they are designed and developed. When you take responsibility for where you want to be, obstacles start to shrink and opportunities multiply.

WHY IS A GAME PLAN APPROACH HELPFUL IN SETTING CAREER GOALS?

It can be overwhelming to think about the career you want 10 years from now when you're staring down the barrel of this week's to-do list. While it's easy to get caught up in the tyranny of the urgent, taking the time to identify what all your hard work is building toward can shift you from surviving to thriving.

Every single career path is different. The road from start to finish is rarely a straight line; it's a winding path with detours and rest stops and hitchhikers and speed limits, both internal and external.

Your Game Plan empowers you to:

1. Identify your ultimate destination.
2. Focus in on the most important next leg of your journey.
3. Map out the actions and resources that will move you forward faster.

In this section, I invite you to spend time identifying the path of least resistance while letting go of routes that no longer serve your goals. This translates as identifying your strengths and weaknesses in order to slowly steer your professional life in the direction of your natural abilities and proclivities.

Each of us has a unique combination of talents, abilities, and experiences. When focused, those qualities flourish, opening doors and connecting you with others who can benefit and build upon them. Doing the work is vital, but discovering the factors that maximize your capabilities comes first.

Wait – but once you discover your passion, shouldn't you make it your career?

I invite you to consider that this line of thinking is backward. First, focus on performing your current job with passion, and then let your career unfold from a place of possibility rather than frustration.

Remember: passion develops. While turning your passion into your career definitely has its benefits, it may take some time to get there. Don't follow your passion to the exclusion of your responsibilities. Your current job may be a learning experience or some much-needed cash, but not the exact thing you were always meant to do, and that's okay. Similarly, many people transform an okay job into a wow job once they're in the door and figure out how to make it their own.

WHAT ARE COMMON OBSTACLES IN SETTING CAREER GOALS?

1. The Blame Game.
It's so easy to play the victim at work. And there are benefits: commiseration bonds you to your coworkers and blaming others gets you out of responsibility for your results.

When things aren't going your way, you have two choices: go to happy hour and complain to your friends, or accept it and find solutions. Which option do you expect will move you toward satisfaction and success?

Perhaps your career goal is to move into a senior management position. But your company only promotes people with an MBA and who kiss up to the boss and dress a certain way and your boss isn't going anywhere plus there's a hiring freeze and the other junior manager has been there longer and no one listens to your ideas and you don't get the good projects and people are dumb because you're super-talented and smarter than the idiots in your department. It's not your fault. You should just call some recruiters and go somewhere you're appreciated, right?

Maybe. Or maybe you do need some more training. Maybe you need to work on your relationship with your boss. Maybe you need to work on communicating your ideas. Maybe your quality of work isn't up to par. Maybe the way you present yourself undermines your professionalism. Maybe you show up at 9:05 and peace out at 5:01 and can't be bothered to go the extra mile. Maybe you should ask to be included in more meetings and special projects. Maybe you need to coherently and objectively write out a strategic plan for fixing what's wrong in your department, enlist your boss's support in executing this plan, and schedule a follow-up evaluation to discuss your performance and your future. And yes, maybe if you try 50 new ways of fixing things and doing your best and still nothing changes, then you do need to go somewhere new.

2. Going for stuff you don't want anymore/isn't important to you now.
It's easy to keep wearing an old goal because you're used to it or someone told you it looked fantastic five years ago. Stop and take an objective look in the mirror: does it really still fit? If you've outgrown your previous Career Vision, give yourself space to create a new one.

Likewise, if it's your year to go full force toward a creative side project or spend maximum time with your kids, it's completely okay to put your career in cruise control. The point is to identify your true priorities shape your goals accordingly.

3. Success-obsessed culture.
We live in a culture that is preoccupied with the pursuit of success. While identifying and pursuing your goals is important, don't strive just for striving's sake. There is nothing wrong with staying in the same job for 20 years if it suits you or with being a stay-at-home parent. I give you full permission to opt out of competing for a job that interferes with your personal goals or the things that give you true happiness and contentment.

Be deliberate in how you build your career and in how it affects the rest of your life. The more conscious you are about what makes you thrive, the more likely you are to connect with your true talent and find satisfaction in your work.

4. Getting too comfortable.
On the flipside, everyone reaches a point where their job situation gets too comfortable for their own good. You hit a plateau. You can perform your role on auto-pilot. Your spouse makes enough money. Your colleagues are also your social circle. Signs you're getting stagnant include phoning in your job duties, getting resentful toward your coworkers, customers, or boss, or acting out in weird ways outside of work, like being more irritable with your family or zoning out to escape rather than to relax.

If you're in a holding pattern, start shaking things up immediately. Take a tiny step – sign onto a small project, rearrange your desk, go to lunch with a new contact – and then use that momentum to motivate yourself toward a larger goal.

WHAT'S THE MOST IMPORTANT THING TO KEEP IN MIND WHEN SETTING CAREER GOALS?

When creating your career Game Plan, be honest about the realities of your work. Clarify what is within your control to change vs. what requires adaptation to systems, people, and the demands of your industry.

STRENGTHS

What are you good at? What do you love to do? What would you do if no one paid you? What would you like to learn? Which professional experiences have you found most rewarding?

NOT SO MUCH

What do you hate to do? When are you not your best? What do you prefer to delegate? Which types of people drain your will to live? Which experiences de-motivate you?

CONTROL

Go back and identify which elements are within your control in your current situation. Are there ways to build in more of your strengths, more of what you find rewarding? Are there ways to delegate or eliminate areas where you don't excel? What is a matter of involving someone else vs. your own attitude or ability adjustment?

BIG PICTURE

Get clear on what you want most by asking:

If everything works out perfectly, what would my career look like one year from now?

Before you write it down, take a few deep breaths and suspend any preoccupation about the How – this is your moment to envision the What.

BRAINSTORM

Now, loosen up and brainstorm everything you want in your career, both short- and long-term. Don't worry about where you are now or that you don't know the steps. Allow yourself to dream and create.

PROJECTS/EXPERIENCES

PEOPLE/RELATIONSHIPS

ACHIEVEMENTS/REPUTATION

COMPENSATION

EDIT

Go back and assign numbers to each goal – how soon do you want to accomplish each? Three months, six months, one year, five years?

Identify which goals depend too much on someone else's actions or permission. Is this goal realistic? Is there a way you can rewrite it to make it mostly within your control?

Group your goals into logical categories – are some of your goals dependent on others? Rewrite your goals here by category, adding goals you may have missed that link the others together. For example, will you have to get a promotion in order to make your salary goal? Do you need to get a certification before you're eligible for that promotion?

PLAY

Go back to your brainstorm pages and pick your top priorities to attack or explore for the next 3-12 months. Note the feeling around each goal – are you inspired and excited? Or do you feel like you have to do it because you should?

Use this page to mess around with the best wording. The final version should be as simple and clear as possible and, above all, be inspiring to **you**.

Write the final version of your goals on the fresh Career Goals page, and then use the pages that follow to create your Game Plan for each one.

GOAL BREAKDOWN

On the following pages, list each goal and be specific about what it will take to accomplish it.

GOAL
What specific, trackable goal will you work toward and accomplish?

Create my professional online presence on my own website and social media by May 30

ADVISORY
Who can contribute solid advice and practical support?

Sarah – has awesome website for her photography business
Barbara – great at resume writing & feedback

RESOURCES
What tools, skills, and other resources do you need and by when will you obtain them?

LinkedIn optimization webinar – by January 15
Copyeditor for my professional bio – by January 30
Web designer or web design template – by February 15

OBSTACLES
What might stand in your way and how will you deal with it proactively?

Too busy/overwhelmed – Schedule two hours per week for this, no interruptions, no exceptions
Don't know how to make a website – Look for a web designer within my budget

POWER QUARTER
What are the major milestones that would have to take place in order to make your big goal a reality? These should be aggressive enough to motivate you, but doable enough to be realized in three months or less. Be specific about its time zone.

Complete amazing personal portfolio that brilliantly showcases my work – Spring (March/April/May)

ACTIONS + DEADLINES
Break down the individual tasks that will help you reach your Quarter Goals. Then go to your calendar and schedule specific times when you will put 100% of your focus on accomplishing these actions.

Ask friends for referrals to good web designers – by March 15
Get comparative quotes from web designers – by April 1
Get endorsement quotes from at least five past clients – by April 1
Update my LinkedIn profile – by April 15

★ CAREER GOALS

CAREER GOAL

GOAL

ADVISORY

RESOURCES

OBSTACLES

POWER QUARTER	ACTIONS + DEADLINES

CAREER GOAL

GOAL

ADVISORY

RESOURCES

OBSTACLES

POWER QUARTER	ACTIONS + DEADLINES

CAREER GOAL

GOAL

ADVISORY

RESOURCES

OBSTACLES

POWER QUARTER	ACTIONS + DEADLINES

CAREER GOAL

GOAL

ADVISORY

RESOURCES

OBSTACLES

POWER QUARTER	ACTIONS + DEADLINES

CAREER GOAL

GOAL

ADVISORY

RESOURCES

OBSTACLES

POWER QUARTER	ACTIONS + DEADLINES

CAREER VISION

It can be incredibly clarifying to unify your goals under a master vision of where you're headed. Your vision is the big-picture stuff: how you feel, who you are, what you're doing, and who you are becoming. It doesn't worry about the how; it focuses on the emotional connection you will feel when you lock into a long-term picture that is fulfilling and uniquely fit for you.

Use this page to formulate the wording that motivates you and matches your personal career aspirations.

Example:
It is September 1, and I feel confident, inspired, and creative. I'm using my talents, including writing, interacting with new people, and being ultra-organized. I love that I have weekends off for the first time in my professional life and I can spend more time with my friends. I've worked through my fear and found opportunity in places I never thought possible. I'm rewarding myself by getting a pair of opera season tickets!

★ CAREER VISION

PROJECT GOALS

★

The project Game Plan is for you if you are in a position of creation or leadership:

PROJECT = Business, Organization, Production, Campaign, Event... **What You're Working On.**
CREATOR = CEO, Owner, Entrepreneur, Coach, Director, Producer, Manager, Artist, Teacher... **You.**

Entrepreneurs, artists, leaders, innovators... we all have one thing in common: vision. What we often need more time and space to develop is the strategy and corresponding plan of action.

HOW ARE PROJECT GOALS DIFFERENT THAN CAREER GOALS?

In project goals, there are usually other people who have a stake in your success. Since your team and your audience have some level of input or interest in how you perform, project goals require an approach that takes this into consideration. Yes, there is often overlap with your career or personal goals, but it's clarifying to understand which elements of your project are yours and which elements are affected by or the responsibility of others.

If you're an entrepreneur, producer, manager, or other in-charge type, I invite you to take this opportunity to create a safe space to go back to basics and be a beginner. Be sure you read The Pregame so you can identify your goal-setting blind spots. Get humble enough to work on your weaknesses and you'll reap the benefits. Paradoxically, you'll also get more respect from those around you.

WHY IS IT IMPORTANT TO SET PROJECT GOALS?

When you're leading a project, it can take 110% of your energy and focus to manage the details. But it is vital to create time and commit resources to working *on* your project, not just *in* your project. To be successful, you must create and define the larger vision and then zero in on your next logical steps.

As a marketing consultant for new businesses and special projects, creators come to me for this perspective. Together we work on everything from competitive positioning to sales strategy to how they're going to finish their first book, and the action plan is different every time. I have never been able to cut and paste one strategy for two different clients, and that's the way it should be.

Those I know who have created profitable businesses, earned awards, raised money, or launched a new product, have indeed celebrated big and well-deserved wins along the way. But behind the scenes, they have also weathered slow months, low-response campaigns, shady competitors, deadbeat partners, outstanding invoices, and the painful moments of self-doubt that sabotage even the most passionate creators.

Successful projects take action, focus, discipline, and the perspective to learn from mistakes. They are a combination of solid strategy and the right team dedicated to hard work over time, which includes the ability to adapt as new opportunities and challenges arise.

WHY IS A GAME PLAN APPROACH HELPFUL FOR SETTING PROJECT GOALS?

A Game Plan empowers you to move past obstacles that sabotage the success of a project:

- Focusing on perfecting a product and neglecting to put equal energy into creating the systems necessary for revenue or sustainability.

- Getting overly distracted by competitors and allowing catch-up actions to sidetrack your strategy.

- Overestimating the effectiveness of what's been done in the past simply because you're used to doing it that way.

- Hiding a fantastic idea with poor planning or lack of promotion.

- Assuming you have to do what everyone else is doing.

- Taking on too much at once and, as a result, none of it gets accomplished.

- Changing your strategy the moment you get bored, scared, or distracted.

- Not asking for outside help when you desperately need support or guidance.

- Giving up too easily when you feel stuck.

All of these are solvable, and it's often easier than you expect. It begins with clarifying why you're in the game, with creating ambitious yet achievable goals, and with identifying a Game Plan to get from here to there.

Your project goals will be set in these six categories:

- **Product.** What do you want to create?
- **Audience.** Who will be impacted most by your project?
- **Money.** How much do you want to invest, raise, or profit?
- **Team.** Who can bring this project to its full potential?
- **Habits.** How do you want to approach your project?
- **Impact.** What reputation are you building?

A Game Plan is not a business plan. A business plan is your long-term, bird's eye view of your project. A Game Plan attacks the immediate and shape strategy around reality, not predictions.

WHAT ARE COMMON OBSTACLES IN SETTING PROJECT GOALS?

While it's important to have long-term vision, it's vital for early-stage creators to know exactly what needs to be done in the next four to twelve weeks. When consulting on new projects, I've stopped constructing annual plans and now create Game Plans: identifying immediate goals and laying out the exact actions, resources, and people it will take to get things done.

In my work launching new projects, I see creators in every industry get stuck, frustrated, or misguided in attempting to apply old models to the new normal. Our current environment moves far too quickly to adhere to traditional methods of forecasting. In just three months, we may be dealing with an entirely different climate, from internal factors like technology and team members to external factors like the economy or new competitors.

WHAT'S THE MOST IMPORTANT THING TO KEEP IN MIND WHEN SETTING PROJECT GOALS?

It's very rare that one single action or opportunity will propel you from development to permanent success. Especially for projects that require an audience – businesses, fundraisers, films, plays, art exhibitions, tournaments, parties, product launches, awareness campaigns – make sure you devote just as much energy to the promotion of your project as you do to its production. Assuming that "if you build it, they will come," may motivate you as a creator, but you'll have to transition from maker to marketer in order to give your project the audience it deserves.

THE DOWNLOAD

Start by assessing where you are now so you can build an ambitious yet realistic plan of action.

PROJECT

NICHE

AUDIENCE

COMPETITORS/COMPETING FACTORS

WHAT ARE YOUR BIGGEST PRIORITIES RIGHT NOW?

IN WHICH AREAS OF YOUR PROJECT DO YOU FEEL THE STRONGEST?

WHAT ARE YOUR PRIMARY CHALLENGES? WHERE COULD YOU USE EXPERT INPUT OR SUPPORT?

VISION

Define success for your project: what would your reality be once it is accomplished?

PRODUCT

AUDIENCE

MONEY

TEAM

HABITS

IMPACT

DELEGATE

What needs to happen internally vs. in-house? If you're building a team, what needs to happen in order to do so – how will you know when it's time to hire? How will you know that you've chosen the right team member? How will you measure the engagement's success?

On the flip side, where might you be pushing off responsibility that actually belongs with you? Are there things you need to tackle in order for your project to be healthy?

RIGHT-SIZE

It's easy to get seduced into project measurement, but let me suggest that it's not size that matters. What matters is how well you work it.

Apply realistic measurement attributes to each goal. How long will it really take? How much do you really need? Is there more than one way to get from here to there?

Narrow down your goals in each category to those that make the most sense to attack first and that can realistically get accomplished within the next three months.

EXPERIMENT

Go back to your Vision page and pick one specific, measurable goal in each area. Use this page to formulate the best wording and make it trackable. The final version should be as simple and clear as possible.

Write the final version of your goals on the fresh Project Goals page, and then use the pages that follow to create your Game Plan for each one.

GOAL BREAKDOWN

On the following pages, list each goal and get specific about what it will take to accomplish it.

GOAL
What do you want to accomplish?

Audience: Build my mailing list to 10,000 subscribers by November 1

ADVISORY
Who can contribute solid advice and practical support?

Claire – specializes in e-newsletter best practices
Kevin – has strong mailing list and can give me tips

RESOURCES
What tools, skills, and other resources do you need and by when will you obtain them?

Contact management account – May 15
Newsletter signup plug-in for my website – June 1

OBSTACLES
What might stand in your way and how will you deal with it proactively?

Not sure if I'm getting enough traffic to my website to get these signups – check Google Analytics
Poor search engine optimization – go through and check my keywords and tags

MILESTONES
What are the major milestones for each goal?

Set up all systems to capture email addresses on website – by May 30
Create strategy and promo materials to get email signups at live events – by June 15

ACTIONS
Break down the individual tasks that will help you reach your milestones, then schedule and commit.

Milestone: Set up all systems to capture email addresses on website – by May 30
Calendar: May Fridays 10am – 12pm
☐ *Research best practices for email signups*
☐ *Repurpose existing worksheet for free gift download with signup*
☐ *Update calls to action in automated confirmation emails*
☐ *Hire Caleb to design and implement site plug-ins*

★ PROJECT GOALS

PRODUCT

GOAL

ADVISORY

RESOURCES

OBSTACLES

PRODUCT

MILESTONES	ACTIONS + DEADLINES

AUDIENCE

GOAL

ADVISORY

RESOURCES

OBSTACLES

AUDIENCE

MILESTONES	ACTIONS + DEADLINES

MONEY

GOAL

ADVISORY

RESOURCES

OBSTACLES

MONEY

MILESTONES	ACTIONS + DEADLINES

TEAM

GOAL

ADVISORY

RESOURCES

OBSTACLES

TEAM

MILESTONES	ACTIONS + DEADLINES

HABITS

GOAL

ADVISORY

RESOURCES

OBSTACLES

HABITS

MILESTONES	ACTIONS + DEADLINES

IMPACT

GOAL

ADVISORY

RESOURCES

OBSTACLES

IMPACT

MILESTONES	ACTIONS + DEADLINES

AFTERPARTY

SUCCESS PRINCIPLES

This is the page to visit when you get stuck. Check your goals and progress against these seven principles; I've found that my solution is usually hanging out in one of these core areas.

1: INTENTION

...What do I really truly want?

Identify that internal itch, that thing that keeps popping up and won't let you ignore it.

2: BELIEF

...Do I fully believe I can achieve it?

Know to your core that you want it and that you can have it. You can absolutely achieve it.

3: PLAN

...Did I create a strong Game Plan?

Write down the goal but also the action steps. You have to write it down. Trust me.

4: DEDICATION

...Am I following my plan with integrity?

Commit to actually follow your plan, even when it's challenging.

5: MEASUREMENT

...Am I tracking my progress?

Record your progress. That way you can see what's working and figure out how to fix what isn't.

6: INSPIRATION

...What will keep me moving forward?

Discover ways to stay connected to your vision, from celebrating milestones to taking a break if needed.

7: CELEBRATION

...What am I looking forward to at the finish line?

Reward yourself and invite others - success is best savored with those you love.

TIME OUT

Here's another way to look at it. Remember: goals are made to be updated and Game Plans are made to be retooled. Just be honest about where you are and why you're there, and then get back into action.

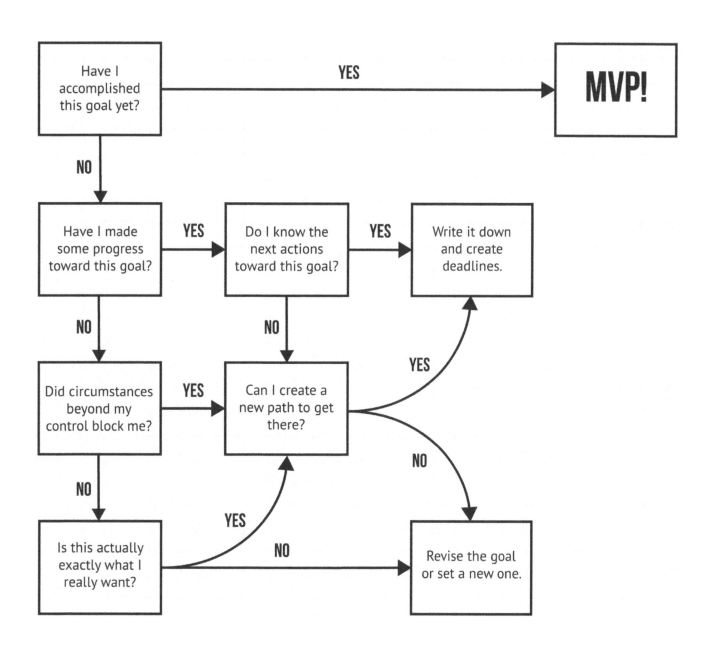

MOTIVATION

The harder you work and the more time you spend pushing out of your comfort zone, the more you'll need to take time out to rest and re-motivate. Use this page to list actions and experiences that help you feel refreshed and optimistic. Be sure to schedule these into your calendar often so you don't burn out.

ACTIVITIES

PLACES

PEOPLE

ALSO

HUDDLE

Be sure to check in with your goals on a regular basis. Schedule a weekly or monthly repeating appointment in your calendar to ask yourself and your team the right questions.

Don't get stressed if you haven't accomplished your goals yet. The point is to assess where you are and how you can best move forward. More importantly, you're on your own team, so evaluating your progress isn't a penalty; it's huddling before the next play.

GOAL

- Are you working toward this goal with 100% integrity?
- Are you doing your personal best?
- Is this still what you want?
- Do you need to reword or retool this goal?
- Do you need to adjust the timeline?
- Are you celebrating milestones and goal achievements?

ACTIONS

- What tools will move you forward?
- Are you missing any resources you need? How and when will you get them?
- Is there another way to your goal?
- What is the next logical small step? When will you take it?
- Who can provide inspiration, advice, or accountability?
- Are your actions just busy work or are they actually moving you forward?
- Can you eliminate any unnecessary actions?

GOAL BUDDY

- Is there any way you can help your buddy with his or her goal?
- Do any of your buddy's goals seem in conflict or out of logical order?
- Are any milestones or actions missing?
- Can you help eliminate an obstacle?
- Can you suggest a contact, resource, or tool?

INFLUENCES

Here is a partial list of people who have influenced my goal-setting process and principles. I encourage you to check out their online content, classes, and books to continue developing your goal approach. I hope the diversity of this list shows that mentors are everywhere – keep your eyes open.

Betsy Capes	Elite career coach for creative professionals and founder of Capes Coaching.
Brené Brown	Human connection researcher, author, and TED talker.
Casey Neistat	Filmmaker with online videos that inspire you to do more.
Cindy Gallop	Brand expert who likes to blow shit up.
Dan Savage	Love, sex, and dating advice that's practical and progressive.
Darbi Worley	Fitness ass-kicker and host of Everything Acting Podcast.
Dave Mowers	Executive coach and corporate trainer specializing in dynamic communication.
Deepak Chopra	Author and guru highlighting the importance of self-care and awareness.
Erin Stutland	Fitness and lifestyle coach with online programs.
Jeff Madoff	Host of private seminar interviewing successful creative entrepreneurs.
Josh Korda	Practical Buddhist teacher at Dharma Punx in New York. Best podcast ever.
Larry Sharpe	Sales trainer and executive coach.
Kate White	Author of straightforward and practical career guides.
Michael Roderick	Networking guru and founder of ConnectorCon events.
Oprah Winfrey	Obviously.
Patricia Moreno	Wellness guru and creator of intenSati, the ultimate mind-body workout.
Pema Chödrön	Author and guru making Buddhism accessible. Every sentence is pure gold.
Sam Chase	That yoga teacher who always says the right thing at the right time.
Sean Carter	Aka Jay Z, plus hip hop in general. Can't knock the hustle.
Sebastian Marshall	Author of *Ikigai* and *Gateless*, strategist with a global perspective.
Suze Orman	Personal finance guru and my tough-love approach mentor.
Tara Mohr	Teaching women how to own their power through wise living.
Vladimir Gerasichev	Elite performance coach on transforming attitudes to shape results.

BOOKS ETC.

These books have also influenced my goal-setting process and approach to life, career, and business success. If you want more guidance in a particular area, I highly recommend the books and authors below. Got more? Send me your favorite resources via Twitter or by emailing Ciara@CiaraPressler.com.

PERSONAL

Augusten Burroughs	**This is How.** A self-help book for people who really want to help themselves.
Barbara Ehrenreich	**Bright-Sided: How Positive Thinking is Undermining America.** Optimism's limits.
Barry Schwarz	**The Paradox of Choice.** When decision matters and when it's best left alone.
Brooks Palmer	**Clutterbusting.** How your stuff reflects your inner life and when to let go.
Don Miguel Ruiz	**The Four Agreements.** Simple truth on how perception shapes reality.
Henrik Edberg	**The Positivity Blog.** Keeping life simple and productive.
M. Scott Peck	**The Road Less Traveled.** A practical approach to life and self-actualization.
Michael Pollan	**Food Rules.** Simple and common-sense nutrition principles.
Oliver Burkeman	**The Antidote: Happiness for People Who Can't Stand Positive Thinking.** Reality.
Sara Eckel	**It's Not You: 27 (Wrong) Reasons You're Single.** You are enough; love is timing.

PROFESSIONAL

Bentley & Urban	**The Savvy Actor Career Manual.** Goal structure for creative professionals.
Fried & Hansson	**Rework.** Keeping business simple and effective, by the founders of 37Signals.
Jack Trout	**Trout on Strategy.** Marketing author whose work helped me avoid business school.
John Bradberry	**The Six Secrets of Startup Success.** Best practices for any entrepreneur.
Michael Gerber	**The E-Myth Revisited.** An entrepreneurial bible on expansion and systemization.
Seth Godin	**The Dip.** When to keep pushing and when to quit.
Tim Ferriss	**The Four-Hour Workweek.** Maximizing your time, ideas, and effort.

SUPPORT

The be-your-best industry has exploded in recent years, and options abound for goal support. It's helpful to understand the different types of support available. As in all things, do your research and comparison shop: what are the options, what do you get for the investment, and what are your advisor's qualifications?

No one will ever know you better than you know yourself, so trust the path that seems the most true to who you are and how you function.

COACH

A coach guides you, but you do the work. A coaching engagement is designed to empower you to act on your own behalf, identify your own blocks, and see your circumstances more clearly. If you're a self-driven person who loves guidance but also wants to learn, coaching may be the right resource for you. The tricky thing about the coaching industry is that it's unregulated – unlike psychology, no degree is required, thus anyone can hang a shingle and declare herself a coach. Ask for references, testimonials, or case studies of others who have been successful after working with the coach or the company.

CONSULTANT

A consultant evaluates your situation and gives you specific guidance on what to do, pointing you in the right direction. If you like to be given a specific plan or to have the work done for you, a consultant is probably your preferred option.

TRAINER

A trainer is a type of consultant. S/he creates a specific plan or curriculum for you to follow in order to get results. If you're social, competitive, or team-oriented, you will probably have an effective learning experience in a group environment.

THERAPIST

If you are constantly holding yourself back and can't figure out why, you might benefit from delving into the depths of your habits and motivations with a licensed professional. Therapy is a safe place with an objective party who has devoted many hours to both the study and practice of the human brain and how it affects the way we behave and believe. As with coaches, try to find a therapist who understands people like you and who comes recommended from a respected source. It's also worth doing a little of your own research on various psychological approaches, i.e., cognitive-behavioral therapy vs. psychoanalytic therapy.

OVERTIME

Now what?! Don't worry, there's more online. Visit my website at www.CiaraPressler.com to get:

EXTRA PAGES

Need more pages to rework your goals or create new ones? Get free downloads, including:

- Personal Goal Game Plan sheets
- Career Goal Game Plan sheets
- Project Game Plan packet
- Success Principles
- If You Only Have a Few Minutes

GOAL EVENTS

Grab your team and host your own goal event – a free DIY Goal Event packet is also online for free download. It includes a sample invitation, event outline, supply list, marketing tips, and a discount on bulk book orders.

I NEED A GAME PLAN

If you're working on a business or professional project, we can work together to build your Game Plan. A customized Game Plan identifies your immediate goals and outlines your action steps.

SEASON TICKETS

Stay tuned for more resources to support your goals – join my email list for the latest advice, events, and content.

MEET THE PRESSLER

I'm Ciara Pressler, a strategist working with businesses and special projects. My personal mission and professional passion are the same: to help people clarify their vision and create an actionable plan to make their goals a reality.

My marketing collective Pressler Collaborative works with projects in entertainment, media, real estate, tech, finance, fitness, lifestyle, and beyond. Before marketing, I was a performer – that career transition was the inspiration for my first book, *Exit Stage Right: The Career Change Handbook for Performers*. I worked on many film, television, and stage projects in New York City as a performer, writer, and producer, including my own play, *Marathon: A Comedy in 26.2 Scenes*.

I continue to create content focused on sharing best practices for marketing, business, and career development. That includes my webseries The Audience, articles on The Huffington Post, and more. I also do guest speaking at conferences, schools, and events on how to be strategic about building your business, career, and professional network.

Let me know what you discover as your goals unfold via Twitter (@TheMayoress) or by emailing Ciara@CiaraPressler.com.

More about my latest work, events, and content, are at www.CiaraPressler.com.

THANK YOU!

KNOW YOURSELF BEFORE YOU GROW YOURSELF

KEEP YOUR GOALS AWAY FROM THE TROLLS

GET SPECIFIC

ACCEPTANCE IS KEY TO KEEP YOU FREE

YOU CAN'T YOLO IF YOU FLY SOLO

RUN YOUR RACE AT YOUR PACE

STRIVE TO PROGRESS NOT OBSESS

SHARE YOUR WEALTH TO STAY IN HEALTH

CHECK YOURSELF BEFORE YOU WRECK YOURSELF	**WHAT COULD HAPPEN IF YOU REMOVED THE EXCUSES?**
WHAT WORKS IN REALITY?	**MOVEMENT BREEDS MOMENTUM BREEDS SUCCESS**
EMOTIONS PASS STICK TO YOUR PLAN	**MAXIMIZE YOUR TALENTS AND OPPORTUNITIES**
BE INVENTIVE NOT PREVENTIVE	**SHOW UP AT 100%**